The Words of the Risen Christ

A Bible Study on Jesus' Resurrection

The Word Among Us Press
7115 Guilford Drive
Frederick, MD 21704
www.wau.org

22 21 20 19 18   6 7 8 9 10

ISBN: 978-1-59325-100-0

Nihil Obstat: Rev. Michael Morgan, Chancellor
Censor Librorum
December 1, 2006

Imprimatur: +Most Rev. Victor Galeone, Bishop of St. Augustine
December 1, 2006

Cover and text design by David Crosson

Vouet, Simon (1590-1649)
The doubting of Saint Thomas. circa 1635-37. Photo: Herve Lewandowski.
Location : Musee des Beaux-Arts, Lyon, France
Photo Credit : Réunion des Musées Nationaux / Art Resource, NY

Made and printed in the United States of America

Library of Congress Control Number: 2006938710

The Words of the Risen Christ

A Bible Study on Jesus' Resurrection

Rich Cleveland

theWORD among us® press

Table of Contents

Introduction

Often when families gather, some time is devoted to reminiscing about our ancestors, our parents, grandparents, and great-grandparents. Mementos are brought out: tintype photos, a baby's crocheted slipper, an aged and yellowed elementary-school essay. We sit and recall what our relatives' lives were like, what they did and what they said, finding in them a glimpse of who we are and a new understanding of what we may be like if we live up to our heritage. Such times anchor our souls, as we recall what was important to those we love.

As Christians, even though we might not have a family history or heritage in which we can find identity and solace, we have been adopted into a wonderful and very real earthly family, one whose roots are anchored in heaven. Our greatest ancestor is none other than the Lord Jesus, who adopted us into the family. The gospels and epistles are the Father's gracious mementos to us, reminding us of what he and his family are like and what he and our forefathers in the faith have said and done, making clear our eternal heritage. The tintypes, crocheted clothing, and yellowed essays pale in importance to this wonderful legacy, especially to what Jesus did and said and believed and instructed. As members of the family of God, we need to consistently delve into Jesus' words and deeds, to meditate on them, and to live what they say, for it is in Jesus that we come to understand who we are as Christians and learn how we are meant to live.

Though every act and word of Jesus is critically important—his incarnation, his life and ministry, his passion and resurrection—in this study we will primarily reflect on the things he said and did with his disciples during the forty days between his resurrection and ascension. These were crucially important days, because Jesus was preparing his followers to be church, to be the family that would carry on his legacy of telling the world about the Father's love and of showing them how to live in harmony with him. During the coming weeks, let us join with the disciples in listening to Jesus' every word. Let's be eager to put our heads together to ponder what Jesus meant and then go to live out his meaning. In doing so, we will anchor our souls and in turn build onto the heritage for future generations.

Here are some practical ways we can make this study fun and enjoyable as well as beneficial and inspiring.

Prepare as though your spiritual life depended on it. Time is too precious and sacred Scripture too valuable to give spiritual formation only a halfhearted effort. As Proverbs advises us,

> My son, if you receive my words
> and treasure up my commandments with you,
> making your ear attentive to wisdom
> and inclining your heart to understanding;
> yes, if you cry out for insight
> and raise your voice for understanding,
> if you seek it like silver
> and search for it as for hidden treasures;
> then you will understand the fear of the LORD
> and find the knowledge of God.
> For the LORD gives wisdom;
> from his mouth come knowledge and understanding. . . .
>
> Then you will understand righteousness and justice
> and equity, every good path;
> for wisdom will come into your heart,
> and knowledge will be pleasant to your soul.
> (Proverbs 2:1-6, 9-10)

A promise so great deserves our best.

Share abundantly from the heart. One of the reasons we study sacred Scripture together is to learn from one another what the Holy Spirit has been teaching us. We believe that Christ dwells in each believer.

When we come together, it is to both listen and share—listening to hear Christ speaking through our friends, and opening our hearts and voices so that Christ might speak through us to our friends.

Here is how Dietrich Bonhoeffer put it:

> God has put this Word into the mouth of men [and women] in order that it may be communicated to other men [and women]. When one person is struck by the Word, he speaks it to others. God has willed that we should seek and find His living Word in the witness of a brother [or sister], in the mouth of a man [or woman]. Therefore, the Christian needs another Christian who speaks God's Word to him. . . . He needs his brother man [sister] as a bearer and proclaimer of the divine word of salvation. (Dietrich Bonhoeffer, *Life Together*)

Think "application" and "implication." Scripture was not given simply to increase our knowledge, but rather to change our lives. It is almost more damaging to study God's words and turn from them without doing anything than not to study sacred Scripture at all. St. James advises,

> [B]e doers of the word, and not hearers only, deceiving yourselves. For if any one is a hearer of the word and not a doer, he is like a man who observes his natural face in a mirror; for he observes himself and goes away and at once forgets what he was like. But he who looks into the perfect law, the law of liberty, and perseveres, being no hearer that forgets *but a doer that acts, he shall be blessed in his doing.* (James 1:22-25; italics added)

As you study, there are two ways you can be affected: first, by the immediate application of God's word to your life, and second, by the future implications of God's word for you. An immediate application, for example, would be to go to a person and ask for forgiveness because, in the midst of your study, the Holy Spirit makes you aware that you have sinned against that person in some way.

God's word may also have broader implications by bringing to your attention the need to think or behave differently in the future— for instance, recognizing that you ought to express thanks more frequently or that you ought to watch television less and become more involved in evangelization. It is easy to forget implications and fail to act on them, so we suggest that you write out a clear statement of what God has impressed you to do. You may also find it helpful to share your resolution with a member of your family or a close friend. Remember, God has promised to bless you in the *doing of it.*

Practical Suggestions:

• Begin your study early in the week so that you have adequate time to think and pray about what you are learning.

• Consider memorizing the words of Psalm 119:33-34 so that you can pray them each week as you begin preparation:

> Teach me, O LORD, the way of thy statutes;
>   and I will keep it to the end.
> Give me understanding, that I may keep thy law
>   and observe it with my whole heart.

• To get the most out of the introductory reflections and the "Reflecting on the Church's Wisdom" sections, instead of simply reading this material, use a pen or pencil to highlight the words and phrases that stand out to you.

• Write out your answers to questions in well-developed paragraphs rather than with just two or three words. Remember, as Dawson Trotman once said, that "thoughts disentangle themselves when they pass through the fingertips."

- Prior to the weekly group meeting, review your study and choose six of the most meaningful things you have learned, so that when you have an opportunity to discuss the material, you will be focused in your sharing.

- Develop meaningful relationships with those in your discussion group by meeting for coffee or a meal. Ask one another questions like, "What has been most meaningful to you about the study we're doing?" or "Where are you in your journey with Christ these days?" You will find that your relationships will be enhanced as you share your life in Christ together.

- Finally, consider making the closing prayer of each session your daily prayer throughout each week of this study.

I am certain that the Lord will richly bless the efforts you put forth to study and share his word. Like the disciples on the road to Emmaus, may God's word burn in your heart as you grow in love and knowledge of him.

Rich Cleveland

Chapter 1

"That the world may know . . . ."

John 17:1-26

1 [Jesus] lifted up his eyes to heaven and said, "Father, the hour has come; glorify thy Son that the Son may glorify thee, 2since thou hast given him power over all flesh, to give eternal life to all whom thou hast given him. 3And this is eternal life, that they know thee the only true God, and Jesus Christ whom thou hast sent. 4I glorified thee on earth, having accomplished the work which thou gavest me to do; 5and now, Father, glorify thou me in thy own presence with the glory which I had with thee before the world was made.

6 "I have manifested thy name to the men whom thou gavest me out of the world; thine they were, and thou gavest them to me, and they have kept thy word. 7Now they know that everything that thou hast given me is from thee; 8for I have given them the words which thou gavest me, and they have received them and know in truth that I came from thee; and they have believed that thou didst send me. 9I am praying for them; I am not praying for the world but for those whom thou hast given me, for they are thine; 10all mine are thine, and thine are mine, and I am glorified in them. 11And now I am no more in the world, but they are in the world, and I am coming to thee. Holy Father, keep them in thy name, which thou hast given me, that they may be one, even as we are one. 12While I was with them, I kept them in thy name, which thou hast given me; I have guarded them, and none of them is lost but the son of perdition, that the scripture might be fulfilled. 13But now I am coming to thee; and these things I speak in the world, that they may have my joy fulfilled in themselves. 14I have given them thy word; and the world has hated them because they are not of the world, even as I am not of the world. 15I do not pray that thou shouldst take them out of the world, but that thou shouldst keep them from the evil one. 16They are not of the world, even as I am not of the world. 17Sanctify them in the truth; thy word is truth. 18As thou didst send me into the world, so I have sent them into the

world. ¹⁹And for their sake I consecrate myself, that they also may be consecrated in truth.

²⁰ "I do not pray for these only, but also for those who believe in me through their word, ²¹that they may all be one; even as thou, Father, art in me, and I in thee, that they also may be in us, so that the world may believe that thou hast sent me. ²²The glory which thou hast given me I have given to them, that they may be one even as we are one, ²³I in them and thou in me, that they may become perfectly one, so that the world may know that thou hast sent me and hast loved them even as thou hast loved me. ²⁴Father, I desire that they also, whom thou hast given me, may be with me where I am, to behold my glory which thou hast given me in thy love for me before the foundation of the world. ²⁵"O righteous Father, the world has not known thee, but I have known thee; and these know that thou hast sent me. ²⁶I made known to them thy name, and I will make it known, that the love with which thou hast loved me may be in them, and I in them."

The resurrection of Jesus and the statements he uttered between his resurrection and his ascension were preceded by the fiery ordeal of the crucifixion. On the night before he died, Jesus had much to say to his disciples. His words, as well as his prayer to his Father, are recorded in John 13–17.

It is important to realize that during this crucifixion-eve discourse, Jesus was fully aware of what he was to encounter after his last earthly meal with his twelve apostles: the betrayal by a beloved friend, the abuse and mockery of a sham trial, and the cruel and lonely death on a cross. Jesus knew that not only he but his disciples as well were facing a decisive moment. The coming ordeal would snuff out his physical life—and would also endanger the spiritual life of his band of followers. As his disciples witnessed the apparent triumph of evil over goodness and of religiosity over truth, they could lose the hope and faith that they had placed in him.

Amazingly, Jesus' thoughts did not turn inward in fear or self-pity; rather, he was concerned for his disciples. His thoughts focused on their well-being, on preserving their faith, and on preparing them for their postresurrection mission.

John 17 provides an indelible impression of Jesus' inner focus and concern as he prayed to the Father for his disciples in what is known as his "high priestly prayer." In summary, Jesus prayed, "Father, . . .

- keep them safe—"keep them in thy name" (17:11);
- keep them united—"that they may all be one; even as thou, Father, art in me, and I in thee" (17:21);
- keep them joyful—"that they may have my joy fulfilled in themselves" (17:13);
- keep them from evil—"keep them from the evil one" (17:15);
- keep them consecrated—"sanctify them in the truth; thy word is truth" (17:17);

- keep them mobilized in mission—"as thou didst send me into the world, so I have sent them into the world" (17:18).

Through this prayer and the words he spoke after the resurrection, Jesus set in place the conditions that would ensure the establishment of the kingdom of God. His disciples were the seed corn of Christianity that, when planted and established, would produce future harvests of souls. Jesus was willing to die for them. And he knew that it was imperative that they be protected and preserved so that they could live for him and advance his kingdom in the post-resurrection world. So, amazing though it may be, in the darkness of that last night, he thought about and prayed for his disciples—and for us as well, for he said, "I do not pray for these only, but also for those who believe in me through their word" (John 17:20).

The realization that Jesus was thinking about us and about our well-being and mission on the eve of his passion can have a profound effect on the way we view life from this point forward. If we have ever wondered about our worth and value, about whether we really matter to God, or whether he cares about our everyday existence, or even whether there is a purpose to our lives, our doubts will dissolve as we read John 17 and listen in on Jesus' intimate conversation with his Father. This prayer is a prayer about you and about me. In it, Jesus entrusts us to the protection of his heavenly Father, to the guidance of the Holy Spirit, to the sanctifying effects of sacred Scripture, and to the impetus of his mission. As the realization of his love and concern starts sinking into our soul, we will respond to Christ with devotion and faithfulness.

Jesus' crucifixion-eve discourse and his high priestly prayer were a prelude to his postresurrection statements. As we will see, these statements will build on the same themes, the same concerns, the same promises, and the same mission that he so passionately spoke about with his Father, the mission for which he was sent into the world—"that the world may know." The importance of both his crucifixion-eve and his postresurrection declarations is heightened by the awareness that these were to be Jesus' last conversations around the momentous events of his passion. Let us not pass over these statements lightly or complete our meditation on them too speedily, lest we miss the impact that God intended Jesus' words to have on us.

▶Learning from Scripture

Jesus' prayer the night before he was crucified gives us wonderful insight into his heart, a revealing summary of his life and ministry, and a prelude to the future focus of the mission he had prepared for us, his church.

Meditatively read Jesus' prayer to his Father in John 17:1-26.

1.   How does Jesus describe his mission?

_____

_____

_____

_____

_____

_____

_____

2.   How does Jesus define eternal life?

_____

_____

_____

_____

_____

_____

_____

3. What do you think is meant by Jesus' use of the word "know" throughout this text?

_____

_____

_____

_____

_____

_____

4. When Jesus speaks of "the world," he most often means an environment that is contrary, hostile, or ambivalent to God.
a. What should be our relationship to the world and our expectations while living in it?

_____

_____

_____

_____

_____

_____

b. What should be our responsibilities?

_____

_____

_____

_____

_____

_____

5. What, specifically, does Jesus desire for his disciples, and, in turn, for us?

    _____

    _____

    _____

    _____

    _____

    _____

    _____

6. What do you learn about prayer by reading Jesus' conversation with the Father?

    _____

    _____

    _____

    _____

    _____

    _____

    _____

▶Reflecting on the Church's Wisdom

In this desolation [mankind's rejection of divine life in Jesus] Jesus turns to the one place where unity is mightier than division and security than doubt: there where the Father commands and the Son obeys; where the Son gives of himself, and the Spirit carries it into human hearts; there where the divine "we" of Father and Son through the Holy Ghost controls all things. Here are Jesus' roots; here is his peace, source of his invulnerable strength and union. From here, the beginning, Jesus departed into the world at his Father's command. Now, in the final hour, the Son tells his Father that he has accomplished the paternal will and glorified him on earth by his obedience.

That Jesus' task "is consummated" must be true because he says so (John 19:30). Yet what a spectacle of failure! His word rejected, his message misunderstood, his commands ignored. None the less, the appointed task is accomplished, through obedience to the death—that obedience whose purity counterbalances the sins of a world. That Jesus delivered his message is what counts—not the world's reaction; and once proclaimed, that message can never be silenced, but will knock on men's hearts to the last day.

—**Romano Guardini,** *The Lord*

Which of Guardini's observations about Jesus speaks most strongly to you right now? Why?

_____

_____

_____

_____

_____

_____

_____

▶ Living the Words of the Resurrection

We all go through times of darkness and pain. Nothing of our experiences compares to what Jesus went through, but they are nonetheless significant to us. We learn from Jesus' example and from prayer that we need to be rooted in the Father's love and will. Then, in times of darkness and pain, we will not be left to rely on our own strength or wallow in self-pity and remorse. Rather, knowing that we are loved, and desiring above all else the Father's will, we can rest in him.

It will be difficult to have this perspective or find consolation in prayer in our moments of need, if in calmer times we do not develop a life of prayer and contemplation. Let us begin today to devote more time to prayer and reflection, so that we may know the Lord more fully, fathom his love more deeply, and discern his will more clearly.

▶Praying in Response to Jesus' Words

Write a prayer to Jesus in response to his loving concern and care for you, as so clearly revealed in John 17.

_____

_____

_____

_____

_____

_____

_____

▶Prayer Together

Pray the following prayer daily during the week prior to discussing this chapter, then close your group discussion by praying it in unison:

". . . That the Lord Jesus will reveal Himself to each one of you, that He will give you the strength to go out and profess that you are Christians, that He will show you that He alone can fill your hearts.

"Accept His freedom and embrace His truth, and be messengers of the certainty that you have been truly liberated through the death and resurrection of the Lord Jesus.

"This will be the new experience, the powerful experience, that will generate, through you, a more just society and a better world.

"God bless you, and may the joy of Jesus be always with you. Amen"

—Pope John Paul II, *A Gift of Enduring Love*

Chapter 2

"Was it not necessary . . . ?"

Luke 24:13-35

[13] That very day two of them were going to a village named Emmaus, about seven miles from Jerusalem, [14]and talking with each other about all these things that had happened. [15]While they were talking and discussing together, Jesus himself drew near and went with them. [16]But their eyes were kept from recognizing him. [17]And he said to them, "What is this conversation which you are holding with each other as you walk?" And they stood still, looking sad. [18]Then one of them, named Cleopas, answered him, "Are you the only visitor to Jerusalem who does not know the things that have happened there in these days?" [19]And he said to them, "What things?" And they said to him, "Concerning Jesus of Nazareth, who was a prophet mighty in deed and word before God and all the people, [20]and how our chief priests and rulers delivered him up to be condemned to death, and crucified him. [21]But we had hoped that he was the one to redeem Israel. Yes, and besides all this, it is now the third day since this happened. [22]Moreover, some women of our company amazed us. They were at the tomb early in the morning [23]and did not find his body; and they came back saying that they had even seen a vision of angels, who said that he was alive. [24]Some of those who were with us went to the tomb, and found it just as the women had said; but him they did not see." [25]And he said to them, "O foolish men, and slow of heart to believe all that the prophets have spoken! [26]Was it not necessary that the Christ should suffer these things and enter into his glory?" [27]And beginning with Moses and all the prophets, he interpreted to them in all the scriptures the things concerning himself.

[28] So they drew near to the village to which they were going. He appeared to be going further, [29]but they constrained him, saying, "Stay with us, for it is toward evening and the day is now far spent." So he went in to stay with them. [30]When he was at table with them, he took the bread and blessed, and broke it, and gave it to them. [31]And

their eyes were opened and they recognized him; and he vanished out of their sight. [32]They said to each other, "Did not our hearts burn within us while he talked to us on the road, while he opened to us the scriptures?" [33]And they rose that same hour and returned to Jerusalem; and they found the eleven gathered together and those who were with them, [34]who said, "The Lord has risen indeed, and has appeared to Simon!" [35]Then they told what had happened on the road, and how he was known to them in the breaking of the bread.

More than once I have been embarrassed to meet someone I should know, but whom I failed to recognize. At those times, I would apologize and search for words, stammering that the problem was with my memory, not with the person's significance to me. For the disciples who didn't recognize their fellow traveler on the road to Emmaus, this embarrassing situation was avoided: just as they finally realized who Jesus was in the breaking of the bread, "he vanished out of their sight" (Luke 24:31).

In this postresurrection appearance, Jesus mildly rebukes Cleopas and his companion for simply not being able to put two and two together and come up with the right answer. For three years he had lived with them and had pointed them to the words of the law and the prophets regarding him and his ministry. For three years he had demonstrated by his words and deeds and miracles that he was the Christ, the one sent from the Father. To their credit the disciples recognized these truths and followed him, yet they did not return to the law and the prophets to find an understanding of Jesus' passion. Instead, they let sorrow and confusion preoccupy their thoughts and dictate their behavior.

Had the disciples simply recalled those passages they knew so well—passages they probably had committed to memory—their fear would have turned to awe and their sorrow to joy. The words of Isaiah 53 and Psalm 22 speak so clearly of what they had just seen Jesus endure, and the promises of Scripture speak so strongly of the triumph that would come from what appeared to be complete disaster. God had not deprived them of this knowledge.

Moreover, Jesus had clearly warned his followers on the same day that his trial was to begin: "A little while, and you will see me no more; again a little while, and you will see me" and "you have sorrow now, but I will see you again and your hearts will rejoice, and no one will take your joy from you" (John 16:16, 22). Through these and other statements, Jesus both warned of the trial and predicted the triumph. He spoke about these things so that his disciples might be kept from "falling away."

It is difficult to imagine how the disciples could be in the actual presence of the resurrected Savior—conversing with him, no less—and yet fail to recognize him. But is it really so hard to believe? We too are often in the actual presence of Jesus but fail to recognize him. When we are with other believers, in whom Jesus lives, he is there, really there. When we read or hear the Scriptures, he is there, really there. When we unite with others around the Eucharist, Christ is present, really present. Yet, sadly, we often fail to recognize him.

But the Lord's loving rebuke, like that of our heavenly Father, is never intended to hurt but only to heal. So we can be confident that he did not, in a snit, abandon the two disciples for failing to remember the teachings of the law and the prophets or for failing to recognize him. Rather, he began walking with them on the path right where they were, pointing out why it *was* necessary for him to die on the cross. Unwilling for them to remain in sorrow, confusion, and ignorance, he opened to them sacred Scripture, which, as they later reported, greatly warmed their hearts. And with great significance, and especially because we believe in his real presence in the Eucharist, "he took the bread and blessed, and broke it, and gave it to them" (Luke 24:30) in a simple meal. At that moment, their eyes were opened and the truth of it all came together: The Lord is risen indeed!

We should take great comfort in this incident. Many of us have experienced sorrow and disappointments that have sometimes left us confused and bewildered, walking aimlessly through life wondering what it is all about. We should find hope that . . .

- Jesus will meet us right where we are;
- he is unwilling to leave us sad, confused, and ignorant;

- through the Holy Spirit, he will readily open the Scriptures to us;
- through sacred Scripture and the Eucharist, we can find both inner warmth and understanding that can change our sorrow and confusion to joy;
- with joy and understanding will come new purpose.

We have a choice: we can remain "foolish and slow of heart to believe" (see Luke 24:25), or we can avail ourselves of the resources that God has so generously given to us? We can become men and women who read and soak up the Scriptures on a deep and regular basis. We can frequently avail ourselves of Jesus' presence in the Eucharist, asking the Holy Spirit to open our understanding. We can allow the Lord to show us why it is often "necessary" to undergo our own trials before we witness God's glory.

This story provides such hope. Let us look at it more closely.

►Learning from Scripture

1. Contrast the psychological makeup of Cleopas and his companion before and after Jesus revealed himself to them.

    _____

    _____

    _____

    _____

    _____

    _____

    _____

2. How do you personally respond to the implications of Luke 24:25, "O foolish men, and slow of heart to believe all that the prophets have spoken"?

_____

_____

_____

_____

_____

_____

3. Identify what the two disciples understood about Christ before he opened the Scriptures to them. What important elements did they not understand?

_____

_____

_____

_____

_____

_____

4. Why was it "necessary" for Christ to suffer these things and to enter into his "glory" (Luke 24:26)?

_____

_____

_____

_____

_____

_____

5. Read and reflect on Isaiah 53 and Psalm 22. If you were one of the disciples on the road to Emmaus, how do you think Jesus would use these passages to refer to himself and his passion?

_____

_____

_____

_____

_____

_____

_____

6. What are some ways in which we can cooperate with Jesus' desire to reveal himself to us through the sacred Scriptures and the Eucharist?

_____

_____

_____

_____

_____

_____

_____

7. What transformation do you expect to see in someone who has come to recognize Jesus?

_____

_____

_____

_____

_____

_____

_____

▶Reflecting on the Church's Wisdom

The Old Testament is an indispensable part of Sacred Scripture. Its books are divinely inspired and retain a permanent value (121).

"The Word of God, which is the power of God for salvation to everyone who has faith, is set forth and displays its power in a most wonderful way in the writings of the New Testament" [*Dei Verbum,* 17] which hand on the ultimate truth of God's Revelation. Their central object is Jesus Christ, God's incarnate Son: his acts, teachings, Passion and glorification, and his Church's beginnings under the Spirit's guidance (124).

"And such is the force and power of the Word of God that it can serve the Church as her support and vigor, and the children of the Church as strength for their faith, food for the soul, and a pure and lasting font of spiritual life." Hence "access to Sacred Scripture ought to be open wide to the Christian faithful" [*Dei Verbum,* 21, 22] (131).

The Church "forcefully and specifically exhorts all the Christian faithful . . . to learn 'the surpassing knowledge of Jesus Christ,' by frequent reading of the divine Scriptures. 'Ignorance of the Scriptures is ignorance of Christ'" [*Dei Verbum,* 25] (133).

—*Catechism of the Catholic Church*

What do these statements imply about the relationship between Scripture and your faith life?

_____

_____

_____

_____

_____

_____

_____

▶Living the Words of the Resurrection

If we want to grow in spiritual understanding and love, Jesus tells us how. His words, reiterated in other passages in Scripture, are summarized succinctly in John 14:21: "He who has my commandments and keeps them, he it is who loves me; and he who loves me will be loved by my Father, and I will love him and manifest myself to him." If we want to learn and understand Jesus' commandments, then we need to study his words in sacred Scripture. If we want to keep his commandments, we need to guard our hearts and ask for the grace to be faithful to him. Because God gives us free will, it is up to us to make the choices that lead us to fulfill his commandments. If we do our part, we will receive what Jesus himself promised us—that we will be loved by the Father and by him, and that he will make himself known to us.

These are lifetime promises, and it's a lifelong process to grasp them. Let's take hold of these promises by developing a plan to spend more time contemplating Jesus' life and words, and by asking the Holy Spirit for his help in doing God's will.

▶Praying in Response to Jesus' Words

Write your own prayer asking Jesus to more fully enable you to know him and his words, and to give you the strength to put his words into practice.

_____

_____

_____

_____

_____

_____

_____

▶Prayer Together

Pray the following prayer daily during the week prior to discussing this chapter, then close your group discussion by praying it in unison:

We pray that the God of our Lord Jesus Christ, the Father of glory, may give us a spirit of wisdom and of revelation in the knowledge of him, having the eyes of our hearts enlightened, that we may know what is the hope to which he has called us, what are the riches of his glorious inheritance in the saints, and what is the immeasurable greatness of his power in us who believe, according to the working of his great might which he accomplished in Christ when he raised him from the dead and made him sit at his right hand in the heavenly places, . . . to him be glory in the church and in Christ Jesus to all generations, for ever and ever. Amen.

—Adapted from Ephesians 1:17-20; Revelation 5:13

Chapter 3

"Peace be with you."

John 20:19-23

[19] On the evening of that day, the first day of the week, the doors being shut where the disciples were, for fear of the Jews, Jesus came and stood among them and said to them, "Peace be with you." [20]When he had said this, he showed them his hands and his side. Then the disciples were glad when they saw the Lord. [21]Jesus said to them again, "Peace be with you. As the Father has sent me, even so I send you." [22]And when he had said this, he breathed on them, and said to them, "Receive the Holy Spirit. [23]If you forgive the sins of any, they are forgiven; if you retain the sins of any, they are retained."

P eace be with you." With these words, the risen Lord greeted his fearful disciples (see John 20:19). This is a familiar expression that we use to greet one another every time we celebrate Mass. But Jesus' words were more than a simple greeting. Rather, with these words he imparted a supernatural serenity and confidence.

Earlier, Jesus had told the apostles that the peace he would leave with them was not the peace of the world, which is fleeting and dependent on circumstances (John 14:27). Instead, his peace would be easily accessible to them, powerful and abiding in the midst of even the most difficult circumstances.

We see how this peace was expressed in the life of Peter after Jesus' resurrection and ascension. Raised in strict Judaism, Peter had maintained its hundreds of laws to the nth degree. So we can only imagine his horror and repugnance when he was instructed in a dream to partake of unclean food and then sent by the Spirit to the house of a gentile centurion, Cornelius. Such actions were counter to all that Peter had been taught and had practiced regarding acceptable spiritual behavior. But in peace of soul, he obeyed God, accepted Cornelius' hospitality, and became instrumental in the conversion of Cornelius and his household (see Acts 10:1-48). Peter also enabled the apostles and other brethren back in Jerusalem—who were just as horrified as Peter had initially been—to realize that God was doing something new by grafting the gentiles into the family of God (see 11:1-18). The peace of Christ reigned in Peter's life.

And, recall for a moment Stephen, surrounded by an angry, screeching, rock-gathering mob (see Acts 7:58). As his body was pelted with stones, he no longer resembled the quaking disciples who, for fear of the Jews, had locked themselves into a room after Jesus' crucifixion (see John 20:19). Even as he was dying, Stephen was a man unafraid, concerned for the souls of his persecutors when he prayed, "Lord

Jesus, receive my spirit. . . . Lord, do not hold this sin against them" (Acts 7:59, 60). Stephen experienced Christ's peace, too.

The peace Jesus gives is real and operational in our hearts because it comes with the Holy Spirit's power. Without this inner peace, we would not be able to respond to his commission to go forth with the message of salvation: "Peace be with you. As the Father has sent me, even so I send you" (John 20:21). Our mission is to proclaim a message of peace—reconciliation between God and man through the mediation of Jesus Christ.

In John 20:22-23, a particular element is introduced into the mission that Jesus gave to his apostles—namely, the ability to forgive a person's sins. All authority was given to Jesus by the Father (see Matthew 28:18; John 5:30), and now he shares that authority with the apostles. As Catholics, we rightly recognize that Jesus was not simply giving this authority to those eleven individuals, to be used only until they died. Rather, we believe that the apostles received this authority on behalf of the church, and that the church is invested with this power until Christ returns.

Along with giving the church the authority to forgive sins, Jesus provides the means to fulfill this commission by giving us the Holy Spirit. Consequently, when the church speaks forgiveness to the world, it does so not on its own authority but rather on Christ's: "Since he is the Son of God, Jesus says of himself, 'The Son of man has authority on earth to forgive sins' and exercises this divine power: 'Your sins are forgiven.' Further, by virtue of his divine authority he gives this power to men to exercise in his name" (*Catechism of the Catholic Church,* 1441).

Jesus, who has all authority, says to the church, Go: "As the Father has sent me, even so I send you" (John 20:21). He empowers the church to obey by saying, "Receive the Holy Spirit" (20:22). He gives the church the authority to guarantee forgiveness: "If you forgive the sins of any, they are forgiven" (20:23). In effect, he says, I send you, I empower you, I authorize you. As members of Christ's church, we are responsible to participate in this mission—to proclaim the message of peace and reconciliation to a world seriously in need of both. Through the power of the Holy Spirit, Jesus wants to give us peace—and he has given us the means to make our peace with him through his body, the church. Are we equipped for the mission? Are we going to take up our joint responsibility to proclaim this good news?

▶Learning from Scripture

1. How "peaceful" do you think the disciples were prior to Jesus' appearance?

    _____

    _____

    _____

    _____

    _____

2. Jesus' words "Peace be with you" were intended to be more than just a pleasant salutation.
    a. How does John 14:25-31 clarify what Jesus means by "peace"?

    _____

    _____

    _____

    _____

    _____

    _____

b. What is the source of this peace?

_____

_____

_____

_____

_____

_____

_____

3. Jesus sent out the disciples just as the Father had sent him (John 20:21). Consider each of the following passages and record one aspect of how the Father sent Jesus:
    a. John 3:16-17

_____

_____

_____

_____

_____

_____

b. John 6:38-39

_____

_____

_____

_____

_____

_____

_____

c. John 8:28-30

_____
_____
_____
_____
_____
_____
_____

d. John 9:4-5

_____
_____
_____
_____
_____
_____

4. In what way(s) do you think God is sending you forth?

_____
_____
_____
_____
_____
_____

5. When you consider this task, to what extent can you identify with the disciples as they are described in John 20:19?

_____

_____

_____

_____

_____

_____

_____

6. What next step can you take to move forward in responding to this commission?

_____

_____

_____

_____

_____

_____

_____

7. What do John 5:30 and Matthew 18:15-22 teach about Jesus' authority and that of the church?

_____

_____

_____

_____

_____

_____

_____

8. How could a greater awareness of the church's authority to forgive sins help you?

_____

_____

_____

_____

_____

_____

_____

▶Reflecting on the Church's Wisdom

Now this power to "forgive sins" Jesus confers through the Holy Spirit upon ordinary men, themselves subject to the snare of sin, namely his apostles: "Receive the Holy Spirit. Whose sins you shall forgive, they are forgiven; whose sins you shall retain, they are retained" (John 20:22-23). This is one of the most awe-inspiring innovations of the Gospel! He confers this power on the apostles also as something which they can transmit—as the church has understood it from the beginning—to their successors, charged by the same apostles with the mission and responsibility of continuing their work as proclaimers of the Gospel and ministers of Christ's redemptive work.

Here there is seen in all its grandeur the figure of the minister of the sacrament of penance who by very ancient custom is called the confessor.

Just as at the altar where he celebrates the Eucharist and just as in each one of the sacraments, so the priest, as the minister of penance, acts "in persona Christi." The Christ whom he makes present and who accomplishes the mystery of the forgiveness of sins is the Christ who appears as the brother of man, the merciful high priest, faithful and compassionate, the shepherd intent on finding the lost sheep, the physician who heals and comforts, the one master who teaches the truth and reveals the ways of God, the judge of the living and the dead, who judges according to the truth and not according to appearances.

This is undoubtedly the most difficult and sensitive, the most exhausting and demanding ministry of the priest, but also one of the most beautiful and consoling. . . . Before the consciences of the faithful, who open up to him with a mixture of fear and trust, the confessor is called to a lofty task which is one of service and penance and human reconciliation. It is a task of learning the weaknesses and falls of those faithful people, assessing their desire for renewal and their efforts to achieve it, discerning the action of the Holy Spirit in their hearts, imparting to them a forgiveness which God alone can grant, "celebrating" their reconciliation with the Father, portrayed in the parable of the prodigal son, reinstating these redeemed sinners in the ecclesial community with their brothers and sisters, and paternally admonishing these penitents with a firm, encouraging and friendly "Do not sin again" (John 8:11).
—**Pope John Paul II,** *Reconciliatio et Paenitentia,* 29

What are some ways you can support the priests you know and encourage vocations to the priesthood? How could this advance the church's mission of peace and reconciliation in the world?

_____

_____

_____

_____

_____

_____

_____

▶Living the Words of the Resurrection

An old Chinese proverb reminds us that "a journey of a thousand miles begins with just one step." Perhaps you are somewhat overwhelmed and bewildered as you reflect on your responsibility to participate wholeheartedly in bringing Jesus' message of peace and reconciliation to the world. It is a daunting task, but as this proverb points out, you simply need to begin by taking the first step. A moving object is always much easier to redirect than a stationary one; so, as you step out, God will guide you to discover your part and to discern how to carry it out.

Looking back on forty-five years of involvement in this mission, I can assure you that there is no greater purpose—and no greater enjoyment—than walking with God day by day and seeing him use us in the lives of others. It is so enjoyable that I cannot even imagine living any other way.

▶Praying in Response to Jesus' Words

Write a prayer in response to Jesus' gift of peace and to his commission, "So I send you."

_____

_____

_____

_____

_____

_____

_____

▶Prayer Together

Pray the following prayer daily during the week prior to discussing this chapter, then close your group discussion by praying it in unison:

Most kind Jesus, grant me your grace, I pray; let it dwell in me, work in me, and abide in me to the end. Grant me always to will and desire whatever is most pleasing and acceptable to You. Let Your will be mine, and let my will ever follow and be conformed wholly to Your own. . . .

Grant me, above all else, to rest in You, that my heart may find its peace in You alone; for You are the heart's true peace, its sole abiding place, and outside Yourself all is hard and restless. In this true peace that is in You, the sole, supreme, and eternal Good, I will dwell and take my rest. Amen.

—**St. Thomas à Kempis,** *The Imitation of Christ*

Chapter 4

*"Do not be faithless,
but believing."*

John 20:24-31

24 Now Thomas, one of the twelve, called the Twin, was not with them when Jesus came. 25So the other disciples told him, "We have seen the Lord." But he said to them, "Unless I see in his hands the print of the nails, and place my finger in the mark of the nails, and place my hand in his side, I will not believe."

26 Eight days later, his disciples were again in the house, and Thomas was with them. The doors were shut, but Jesus came and stood among them, and said, "Peace be with you." 27Then he said to Thomas, "Put your finger here, and see my hands; and put out your hand, and place it in my side; do not be faithless, but believing." 28Thomas answered him, "My Lord and my God!" 29Jesus said to him, "Have you believed because you have seen me? Blessed are those who have not seen and yet believe."

30 Now Jesus did many other signs in the presence of the disciples, which are not written in this book; 31but these are written that you may believe that Jesus is the Christ, the Son of God, and that believing you may have life in his name.

Contrary to what some may think, the old adage "seeing is believing" doesn't always hold true. C. S. Lewis tells the story of a woman who swears to have seen a ghost. But, when asked if she believes in the supernatural, she denies it. Similarly, most of us have seen wonderful illusionists who supposedly do masterful feats, yet we don't believe them to be real even though they appear to be so. Rather, we believe them to be just what they are—tricks.

Many of us identify with the disciple Thomas in this scene from John's gospel not because we need to see to believe, but because someone or something has undermined our confidence and caused us to question our faith. Thomas was not wrestling with atheism or considering abandoning his faith in God; he simply found it hard to believe that Jesus bodily rose from the dead, which is a cornerstone of our faith. Perhaps, too, Thomas' remarks simply reflected his disappointment that he had not been there when the risen Lord appeared to the other apostles.

All people have faith. All people believe, even atheists. The question is not "Do you believe?" but "In whom do you believe?" The atheist, rather than believing in God, who has manifested himself in word and deed, chooses to rely on his own reasoning and believe that there is no God.

Jesus' statement "Do not be faithless, but believing" (John 20:27) is addressed to each of us, firm believers as well as atheists and those wrestling with issues of faith. We have a choice, for faith is first and foremost an act of the will, and only secondarily an act of knowing. Jesus said, "My teaching is not mine, but his who sent me; *if any man's will is to do his will, he shall know* whether the teaching is from God or whether I am speaking on my own authority" (7:16-17; italics added).

Do you remember when Jesus said that he was not only praying for the twelve disciples, "but also for those who believe in me through their word" (John 17:20)? In this encounter with Thomas, Jesus is thinking of you and me once again, and pronounces a blessing on us: "Blessed are those who have not seen and yet believe" (20:29). Unlike Thomas, who would only believe when he could see and feel Jesus' wounds, other early believers loved Jesus and believed that he had risen from the dead even though they had never seen him physically. Was this easier for them than for us? No! It still took faith and commitment. And, like the early Christians, when we reaffirm our love and faith in Christ, the Holy Spirit will respond to our receptivity, and like a breath from heaven that blows on the embers of our faith, he will reignite our enthusiasm and confidence.

We cannot fault Thomas—he was not so unlike many of us who have struggled with faith issues. Rather, he is a saint whose faith we can imitate. For when his eyes were opened—yes, even before he reached forth his hand and touched the risen savior—Thomas professed his belief, "My Lord and my God!" (John 20:28). There was now no doubt in Thomas' mind. Having been "willing to do God's will," he now *knew* with a certainty.

We would all love to see Jesus in the flesh in our lifetime, to behold his face, to see his scars, and to talk with him. But in his wisdom and mercy, he chose a better way to always be with us by leaving us his indwelling presence—his presence in the Eucharist, and the Holy Spirit. So, like Thomas, each of us can experience Jesus' presence personally. Thanks be to God for his unspeakable gift!

▶Learning from Scripture

1. In what ways are you able to identify with Thomas?

    _____

    _____

    _____

    _____

    _____

    _____

    _____

2. According to this passage, what should be the basis of our faith?

    _____

    _____

    _____

    _____

    _____

    _____

    _____

3. How would you describe Jesus' treatment of Thomas' doubts? What insight does it give you about Jesus?

    _____

    _____

    _____

    _____

    _____

    _____

    _____

4. Read the account of Jesus' encounter with the Samaritan woman in John 4:1-39.

a. Describe the progression of faith in her life, and in the lives of her fellow Samaritans, from nonbelief to belief.

_____

_____

_____

_____

_____

_____

_____

b. What elements influenced the faith of these Samaritans?

_____

_____

_____

_____

_____

_____

5. Though you may have been baptized as an infant, at some point in your journey to adulthood you had to both affirm and confirm your faith. What influenced you to have faith?

_____

_____

_____

_____

_____

_____

6. Jesus blesses those who believe even though they have not seen proof of his resurrection. Read Romans 10:8-17.
a. Reflect on verses 8-13 and define in your own words what it means to believe.

_____

_____

_____

_____

_____

_____

_____

b. In light of verses 14-17, what is our responsibility for maintaining the quality of our faith?

_____

_____

_____

_____

_____

_____

_____

▶Reflecting on the Church's Wisdom

The one word faith can have two meanings. One kind of faith concerns doctrines. It involves the soul's ascent to and acceptance of some particular matter. It also concerns the soul's good, according to the words of the Lord: whoever hears my voice and believes in him who sent me has eternal life, and will not come to be judged. And again: he who believes in the Son is not condemned, but has passed from death to life.

How great is God's love for men! Some good men have been found pleasing to God because of years of work. What they achieved by working for many hours at a task pleasing to God is freely given to you by Jesus in one short hour. For if you believe that Jesus Christ is Lord and that God raised him from the dead, you will be saved and taken up to paradise by him, just as he brought the thief there. Do not doubt that this is possible. After all, he saved the thief on the holy hill of Golgotha because of one hour's faith; will he not save you too since you have believed?

The other kind of faith is given by Christ by means of a special grace. . . . Now this kind of faith, given by the Spirit as a special favor, is not confined to doctrinal matters, for it produces effects beyond any human capability.

—**St. Cyril of Jerusalem,** from a catechetical instruction, *The Liturgy of the Hours*

What conclusions about faith would you draw from this selection by St. Cyril?

_____

_____

_____

_____

_____

_____

▶Living the Words of the Resurrection

Have you ever wondered whether you will make it to heaven? Many Christians experience struggles regarding assurance of their salvation. Invariably, this insecurity arises because we are looking at the nature of our faith rather than at the object of our faith—Jesus. Or, it can surface because we are aware that our behavior contradicts our faith, and we wonder whether our faith is real.

We gain confidence when we put into practice this advice from the author of Hebrews: "Let us also lay aside every weight, and sin which clings so closely, and let us run with perseverance the race that is set before us, looking to Jesus the pioneer and perfecter of our faith, who for the joy that was set before him endured the cross, despising the shame, and is seated at the right hand of the throne of God" (Hebrews 12:1-2). As we continue to love and follow Christ, we can be free of fear and confident in his mercy and faithfulness to bring us to eternal life. We should never doubt that he is utterly reliable.

▶Praying in Response to Jesus' Words

Write a prayer to the Father about your faith, and perhaps your doubts, too.

_____

_____

_____

_____

_____

_____

_____

▶Prayer Together

Pray the following prayer daily during the week prior to discussing this chapter, then close your group discussion by praying it in unison:

Lord, I believe:
> I wish to believe in Thee.

Lord, let my faith be full and unreserved,
> and let it penetrate my thought,
> my way of judging Divine things and human things.

Lord, let my faith be joyful
> and give peace and gladness to my spirit,
> and dispose it for prayer with God
> and conversation with men,
> so that the inner bliss of its fortunate possession
> may shine forth in sacred and secular conversation.

Lord, let my faith be humble and not presume
> to be based on the experience of my thought and of my feeling;
> but let it surrender to the testimony of the Holy Spirit,
> and not have any better guarantee
> than in docility to Tradition
> and to the authority of the *magisterium* of the Holy Church.

Amen.

> **—Pope Paul VI,** Prayer for Faith

Chapter 5

"Come and have breakfast."

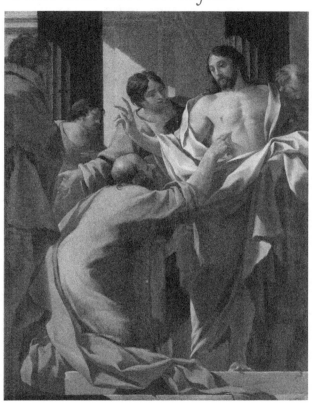

John 21:1-14

¹ After this Jesus revealed himself again to the disciples by the Sea of Tiberias; and he revealed himself in this way. ²Simon Peter, Thomas called the Twin, Nathanael of Cana in Galilee, the sons of Zebedee, and two others of his disciples were together. ³Simon Peter said to them, "I am going fishing." They said to him, "We will go with you." They went out and got into the boat; but that night they caught nothing.

⁴ Just as day was breaking, Jesus stood on the beach; yet the disciples did not know that it was Jesus. ⁵Jesus said to them, "Children, have you any fish?" They answered him, "No." ⁶He said to them, "Cast the net on the right side of the boat, and you will find some." So they cast it, and now they were not able to haul it in, for the quantity of fish. ⁷That disciple whom Jesus loved said to Peter, "It is the Lord!" When Simon Peter heard that it was the Lord, he put on his clothes, for he was stripped for work, and sprang into the sea. ⁸But the other disciples came in the boat, dragging the net full of fish, for they were not far from the land, but about a hundred yards off.

⁹ When they got out on land, they saw a charcoal fire there, with fish lying on it, and bread. ¹⁰Jesus said to them, "Bring some of the fish that you have just caught." ¹¹So Simon Peter went aboard and hauled the net ashore, full of large fish, a hundred and fifty-three of them; and although there were so many, the net was not torn. ¹²Jesus said to them, "Come and have breakfast." Now none of the disciples dared ask him, "Who are you?" They knew it was the Lord. ¹³Jesus came and took the bread and gave it to them, and so with the fish. ¹⁴This was now the third time that Jesus was revealed to the disciples after he was raised from the dead.

How do you deal with disappointment and frustration? What do you do when a dream dies, when you lose confidence in yourself and in life?

We don't know all that was going on in the disciples' hearts and minds after Jesus' crucifixion, but it is not unreasonable to think that Peter was feeling shattered and empty. His best friend, the one to whom he swore undying allegiance, had been unjustly tried as a criminal and brutally executed. Along with the shattering of Peter's dreams about the establishment of the kingdom of God must also have come the shattering of his self-respect as he recalled his cowardly denial of Jesus. But since the evening when Peter had seen the risen Lord appear to him and the other disciples as they were gathered together in Jerusalem, he surely must have been wondering how Jesus would respond if he were given the chance to talk with him one on one.

At times of anxiety people often seek escape from realities that are too difficult to bear. Perhaps when Peter announced, "I am going fishing" (John 21:3), he was seeking just such an escape, a way to occupy his time and thoughts. Or, perhaps he was harking back to that wonderful day when Jesus first called him away from his nets and fishing business with the invitation, "Follow me, and I will make you fishers of men" (see Matthew 4:18-20 and Luke 5:1-11). Had it all gone awry with his denial of Jesus? Surely it must have seemed so in Peter's mind.

But life in Christ is not designed to be lived alone. For it is in times of isolation that the downward spiral of disappointment, doubt, discouragement, depression, and despair accelerates. It is in times of darkness that the faith and hope of our brothers and sisters in Christ can and should bring us the light of Christ. So when Peter announced, "I am going fishing," his companions aptly said, "We will go with you" (John 21:3). They were there to share in Peter's life, and to be available to him and to each other.

More important, Jesus' appearance on the shore of the Sea of Tiberias underscored the central reality of Christian community: Jesus is always with us, not only in the good times of peace and joy, but also in our pain and sorrow. Even in our moral failures he seeks us out and ministers to our woundedness. He makes himself uniquely present to us in the lives of our companions and fellow believers, as well as in the Eucharist and the sacraments. He is ever present through his indwelling Spirit. This is the nature of the one God sent into the world (see John 3:17; 5:36): he seeks out those who feel lost and alone.

In the gospel accounts of Jesus' life, we see how much his ministry revolved around shared meals. Some meals were simple, others elaborate. Some were with friends, others with strangers. Some were with saints, others with sinners. Yet all the meals Jesus shared with others had one thing in common: each was an invitation to friendship with the Son of God. As one biblical scholar points out,

> Meals, even the most ordinary, reach their highest expression in sacramental self-offering and communion. Every Christian meal reveals aspects of the kingdom of God, where guests are welcome, people share with one another, broken covenants are renewed, and all are reconciled. (Eugene LaVerdiere, *Dining in the Kingdom of God*)

Jesus' disciples inherently recognized the significance of sharing this lakeside meal with him. They were seeking fish, and Jesus was seeking them. The risen Lord confronted his friends' sorrow and toil with his own power and abundance, and the apostles jumped for joy—literally, in Peter's case, as he sprang into the water to reach Jesus (see John 21:7). By the time they returned to shore with their nets nearly torn by the miraculous haul of fish, Jesus already had a charcoal fire burning in preparation for breakfast. As the Lord matched the abundance of the catch with the abundance of his love, he restored community with Peter and his disciples—and their hope, as well.

May we come to recognize that the risen Lord is ever present to invite us into community with him: to experience life, reconciliation, and mission. And may we realize, too, that Christ's invitation is often encountered through one another, as we learn to give and receive love and forgiveness.

▶Learning from Scripture

1. Read Luke 5:1-11, the description of Peter's first fishing encounter with Jesus, and compare it with this postresurrection encounter in John 21:1-14, 19.
    a. What similarities and differences do you see in the two occasions?

    _____

    _____

    _____

    _____

    _____

    _____

    b. In each experience it seems that Peter was the one who was most responsive outwardly. What do you think Peter's responses indicate about him in each encounter? About his view of Jesus?

    _____

    _____

    _____

    _____

    _____

    _____

c. What truth(s) do you think Jesus is trying to communicate in each shoreline encounter by providing such an abundant catch?

_____

_____

_____

_____

_____

_____

2. What do the disciples teach us about community through their interactions with Jesus and with one another in the postresurrection scene along the shore?

_____

_____

_____

_____

_____

_____

3. 1 Corinthians 12:20-27 and Philippians 2:1-5 provide insight into how we are to relate in community.
a. What is the gist of these passages?

_____

_____

_____

_____

_____

_____

_____

b. In a parish of hundreds, it can be difficult to experience community with everyone. Where do you personally provide and find community?

_____

_____

_____

_____

_____

_____

_____

4. Why do you think sharing meals promotes friendship and intimacy? How have you experienced community from gathering over meals with others?

_____

_____

_____

_____

_____

_____

_____

5. Read and reflect on Luke 22:14-20. In light of the Last Supper, what significance do you associate with Jesus' postresurrection invitation "Come and eat"?

_____

_____

_____

_____

_____

_____

6. What should be our expectations each time we respond to Jesus'
    eucharistic invitation, "Come and eat?" What effect should it
    have on our anxiety, our guilt, or our relationships?

    _____

    _____

    _____

    _____

    _____

    _____

    _____

    _____

▶Reflecting on the Church's Wisdom

Jesus says to Peter: "*Duc in altum*—Put out into the deep" (Luke
5:4). Peter and the first companions trusted Christ's words and
cast their nets. . . .

"*Duc in altum!*" The command of Christ is particularly rel-
evant in our time, when there is a widespread mentality which,
in the face of difficulties, favors personal non-commitment. The
first condition for "putting out into the deep" is to cultivate a deep
spirit of prayer nourished by a daily listening to the Word of God.
The authenticity of the Christian life is measured by the depth of
one's prayer, an art that must be humbly learned "from the lips
of the Divine Master," almost imploring "like the first disciples:
'Lord, teach us to pray!' (Luke 11:1). In prayer, a conversation
with Christ develops and it makes us his intimate friends: 'Abide
in me and I in you' (John 15:4)" (*Novo millennio ineunte*, 32).

The link with Christ through prayer also makes us aware that
he is also present in moments of apparent failure, when tireless
effort seems useless, as happened to the Apostles themselves,
who after toiling all night, exclaimed: "Master, we took nothing"
(Luke 5:5). It is especially in these moments that one needs to

open one's heart to the abundance of grace and to allow the word of the Redeemer to act with all its power: *"Duc in altum!"*

—Pope John Paul II, Message for the 42nd World Day of Prayer for Vocations, 11 August 2004

In what ways has Jesus called you to "put out into the deep"? How have you responded?

_____

_____

_____

_____

_____

_____

_____

▶ Living the Words of the Resurrection

I remember a couple of times when I responded to a hard day or a disappointment by sliding into an unsociable pique for several days. Then Sunday morning dawned on me—no pun intended—and I was faced with the question of what I was going to do about receiving Christ in the Eucharist. I knew that I could not receive Christ if I was not reconciled to him and to others as well. So, before arriving at church, I had to turn to my family and ask forgiveness. I'm thankful that Jesus established a meal that both brings and requires reconciliation. Shouldn't every meal do the same?

Jesus tells us that we should be reconciled before we worship (Matthew 5:24). Inasmuch as the home is a form of domestic church, shouldn't each meal provide the same kind of check and balance on our relationship with other family members? No reconciliation, no food?

▶Praying in Response to Jesus' Words

Write your own prayer in response to Jesus' invitation "Ccme and eat."

_____

_____

_____

_____

_____

_____

_____

▶Prayer Together

Pray the following prayer daily during the week prior to discussing this chapter, then close your group discussion by praying it in unison:

Jesus, Son of God,
    in whom the fullness of the Divinity dwells,
    you call all the baptized to "put out into the deep,"
    taking the path that leads to holiness.
    Waken in the hearts of each of us the desire
    to be witnesses in the world of today
    to the power of your love.
    Fill us with your Spirit of fortitude and prudence,
    so that we may be able to discover the full truth
    about ourselves and our own vocation.

Our Savior,
    sent by the Father to reveal his merciful love,
    give to your church the gift
    of people who are ready to put out into the deep,
    to be the sign among their brothers
    of your presence which renews and saves.
Holy Virgin, Mother of the Redeemer,
    sure guide on the way towards God and towards neighbor,
    you who pondered his word in the depth of your heart,
    sustain with your motherly intercession
    our families and our ecclesial communities,
    so that they may help people
    to answer generously the call of the Lord.
Amen.

    —Pope John Paul II, Message for the 42nd World Day of Prayer for Vocations, 11 August 2004

Chapter 6

"Do you love me?"

John 21:15-19

¹⁵ When they had finished breakfast, Jesus said to Simon Peter, "Simon, son of John, do you love me more than these?" He said to him, "Yes, Lord; you know that I love you." He said to him, "Feed my lambs." ¹⁶A second time he said to him, "Simon, son of John, do you love me?" He said to him, "Yes, Lord; you know that I love you." He said to him, "Tend my sheep." ¹⁷He said to him the third time, "Simon, son of John, do you love me?" Peter was grieved because he said to him the third time, "Do you love me?" And he said to him, "Lord, you know everything; you know that I love you." Jesus said to him, "Feed my sheep. ¹⁸Truly, truly, I say to you, when you were young, you girded yourself and walked where you would; but when you are old, you will stretch out your hands, and another will gird you and carry you where you do not wish to go." ¹⁹(This he said to show by what death he was to glorify God.) And after this he said to him, "Follow me."

Before their breakfast encounter with the risen Lord on the lakeshore, the Passover meal was the last time the disciples had eaten with Jesus. It was there in that upper room that Jesus had prepared a meal within the meal: he took the common bread and wine of the Passover meal and offered it as the meal of his body and blood, the body and blood of a new and everlasting covenant for the forgiveness of sins.

That same night, Jesus was betrayed. We must keep in mind that Jesus' betrayal was not only Judas' notorious act or Peter's denial, but also the dreadful abandonment of Jesus by all of his disciples (though John later stood with him at the cross). Surely, the disciples must have experienced some residual guilt for having abandoned Jesus. The disciples must have been filled with joy to know that their Lord had prepared another meal for them here on the shore. As he broke the bread and distributed it to them along with some fish, how they must have rejoiced as they remembered that previous meal, when he assured them of forgiveness while distributing the bread of his body and the wine of his blood. In spite of past sins and failures, communion with Jesus was possible, all because of his provision and grace.

Between the time when the disciples responded to Jesus' invitation to come and eat and his personal conversation with Peter, one wonders what the disciples and Jesus talked about. Did they discuss the last few hours of his life prior to the crucifixion, or did they speak of the future of his kingdom? Did they share their fear of the Jews, or just their love of Jesus' presence? Above all, one wonders what thoughts the apostles—and especially Peter—may have kept to themselves.

If you have ever felt really guilty about something you did or said, you know of the internal agony experienced long after the wrongful incident has passed. Did Peter remember with embarrassment and regret his boast, "Lord, I am ready to go with you to prison and to death" (Luke 22:33)—or did he just keep recalling with angst the crowing of the rooster? In all likelihood, either as he sat there at breakfast by the lake or earlier at Jesus' first resurrection encounter with his apostles, he had said, "Lord, I am so sorry, so sorry that I let you down when I should have stood with you. So sorry that I denied you." Yet, Peter was still unsettled in his heart and still needed closure to that unfortunate failure. He still needed to know that all was made right.

Three times Jesus asked Peter the same question, "Do you love me?" With each assurance by Peter, "Yes, Lord," Jesus affirmingly replied, "Feed my sheep" (John 21:15-17). Jesus further assured Peter of the significance of his future contribution by indicating how Peter would die in service to God's glory. Finally, Jesus said to Peter, "Follow me" (21:19), once again offering to Peter a lifetime of companionship with him in mission. Communion was now complete for Peter, forgiveness fully experienced, and purpose fully restored.

Throughout Scripture Jesus' mission is called a mission of "reconciliation" (2 Corinthians 5:18) in which both peace and purpose are restored (Ephesians 2:13-22). As Peter ate breakfast with Jesus and some of his fellow fishermen-disciples, Jesus enabled Peter to recognize and affirm both his love for the Master and Jesus' love for him. In addition, Peter experienced a recall: not the recall of a defective part, but another call to follow and serve Jesus, just as if his denial had never happened. This is what reconciliation is all about, removing barriers and restoring our relationship with God.

▶Learning from Scripture

1. In your life in Christ, what have you learned about spiritual estrangement and reconciliation?

    _____

    _____

    _____

    _____

    _____

    _____

    _____

2. Read and reflect on Luke 22:28-34.
    a. What does this prediction of Peter's denial tell you about Peter? What does it tell you about Jesus' attitude toward Peter?

    _____

    _____

    _____

    _____

    _____

    _____

    _____

    b. How can this passage help you deal with your own failures as a follower of Jesus?

    _____

    _____

    _____

    _____

    _____

    _____

3. Jesus asked Peter, "Do you love me more than these?" (John 21:15).
   a. What or whom do you think Jesus was referring to when he used the word "these"?

   _____

   _____

   _____

   _____

   _____

   _____

   _____

   b. Who, or what, constitute "these" in your life?

   _____

   _____

   _____

   _____

   _____

   _____

   _____

4. What parallels do you see between Peter's denial in Luke 22:54-63 and this lakeshore conversation between Jesus and Peter?

   _____

   _____

   _____

   _____

   _____

   _____

   _____

5. What do you think Jesus was trying to accomplish by his questions to Peter in John 21:15-17?

_____

_____

_____

_____

_____

_____

6. What do you think the other disciples were thinking as they heard Jesus' conversation with Peter?

_____

_____

_____

_____

_____

_____

7. In light of the description of a shepherd's concerns for his sheep in Ezekiel 34:11-15, 23, what does Peter's love for Jesus have to do with feeding Jesus' sheep?

_____

_____

_____

_____

_____

_____

8. After reflecting on Jesus' words in Luke 9:22-27 as well as those in John 21:19-22, describe what it means to "follow me?"

    _____

    _____

    _____

    _____

    _____

    _____

    _____

9. Where do you see yourself in this lakeshore encounter with the risen Lord?

    _____

    _____

    _____

    _____

    _____

    _____

▶Reflecting on the Church's Wisdom

The power of God the Father and God the Son is at work in the whole of creation. The saints are those who are fully receiving life in the Holy Spirit. Accordingly it is said, "no man can say that Jesus is Lord except in the Holy Spirit." However unworthy the apostles might have been, they were told: "You shall receive power when the Holy Spirit is come upon you." This is what is referred to by the phrase, "he who has sinned against the Son of Man is worthy of forgiveness." Even if one at times ceases to live according to this divine word, even if one falls into ignorance or folly, the way is not blocked to true penitence and forgiveness.

—**Origen,** "On First Principles I.3," *Ancient Christian Commentary on Scripture*

In what ways do Origen's observations apply to your own life?

_____

_____

_____

_____

_____

_____

_____

▶Living the Words of the Resurrection

Perhaps you have read this scene and are now thinking, "I've really blown it. By my actions and attitudes I have squelched Jesus' power and presence in my life." Well, cheer up! This is where God triumphs over our own ways of thinking and acting. Through confession and forgiveness, the slate can be wiped clean. You can stand justified before God—just as if you had never sinned.

To conclude this section, do a little research on your diocesan Web site or in the phone book to learn the times and locations where the Sacrament of Reconciliation is offered. Then look at your calendar and determine a date and time to reflect, repent, and receive reconciliation. Remember the words of Origen: "The way is not blocked to true penitence and forgiveness."

▶Praying in Response to Jesus' Words

Write your own prayer in answer to Jesus' question, "Do you love me?"

_____

_____

_____

_____

_____

_____

▶Prayer Together

Pray the following prayer daily during the week prior to discussing this chapter, then close your group discussion by praying it in unison:

Have mercy on me, O God,
    according to thy steadfast love;
    according to thy abundant mercy
        blot out my transgressions.
Wash me thoroughly from my iniquity,
    and cleanse me from my sin!
For I know my transgressions,
    and my sin is ever before me. . . .
Behold, thou desirest truth in the inward being;
    therefore teach me wisdom in my secret heart.
Purge me with hyssop, and I shall be clean;
    wash me and I shall be whiter than snow.
Fill me with joy and gladness. . . .
Hide thy face from my sins,
    and blot out all my iniquities.
Create in me a clean heart, O God,
    and put a new and right spirit within me. . . .
Restore to me the joy of thy salvation.
    —David's Prayer of Repentance, Psalm 51:1-3, 6-8, 9-10, 12

Chapter 7

"I send the promise of my Father upon you."

Luke 24:36, 44-53

[36] Jesus himself stood among [his disciples]. . . . [44]Then he said to them, "These are my words which I spoke to you, while I was still with you, that everything written about me in the law of Moses and the prophets and the psalms must be fulfilled." [45]Then he opened their minds to understand the scriptures, [46]and said to them, "Thus it is written, that the Christ should suffer and on the third day rise from the dead, [47]and that repentance and forgiveness of sins should be preached in his name to all nations, beginning from Jerusalem. [48]You are witnesses of these things. [49]And behold, I send the promise of my Father upon you; but stay in the city, until you are clothed with power from on high."

[50] Then he led them out as far as Bethany, and lifting up his hands he blessed them. [51]While he blessed them, he parted from them, and was carried up into heaven. [52]And they worshiped him, and returned to Jerusalem with great joy, [53]and were continually in the temple blessing God.

Acts 1:3-9

³ To [his disciples] he presented himself alive after his passion by many proofs, appearing to them during forty days, and speaking of the kingdom of God. ⁴And while staying with them he charged them not to depart from Jerusalem, but to wait for the promise of the Father, which, he said, "you heard from me, ⁵for John baptized with water, but before many days you shall be baptized with the Holy Spirit."

⁶ So when they had come together, they asked him, "Lord, will you at this time restore the kingdom to Israel?" ⁷He said to them, "It is not for you to know times or seasons which the Father has fixed by his own authority. ⁸But you shall receive power when the Holy Spirit has come upon you; and you shall be my witnesses in Jerusalem and in all Judea and Samaria and to the end of the earth." ⁹And when he had said this, as they were looking on, he was lifted up, and a cloud took him out of their sight.

The incarnation and the ascension of the Lord—events that mark the beginning and the end of his life on earth—proclaim the same message: Jesus is sent from heaven. More than forty-five times in the Gospel of John alone, reference is made to this fact. If this were not so, people could claim that the good news was just another religious philosophy devised by a clever man. However, not only Jesus' incarnation and ascension but his resurrection appearances as well, in which "he presented himself alive after his passion by many proofs" (Acts 1:3), attest to the fact that he is the "Sent One." This knowledge was essential for Jesus' disciples in light of the worldwide mission they were to embrace and the worldwide persecution they were to encounter.

Jesus' ascension was also necessary for his presence to remain with his disciples at all times and for all time. Jesus said, "I tell you the truth: it is to your advantage that I go away, for if I do not go away, the Counselor will not come to you; but if I go, I will send him to you" (John 16:7). The ascension was the means through which the Holy Spirit came to us. And through the coming of the Holy Spirit, the indwelling of God in us was made possible forever. From that point on, the apostles spoke of "Christ in you" (Colossians 1:27) when referring to the life of his followers, and of living "as Christ" when speaking of their behavior (see 2:6; Ephesians 4:32; 5:2). It is only by the Holy Spirit's indwelling presence that both our position in Christ and our power to live as Christ's body are possible.

The Holy Spirit, the "promise of the Father" (Luke 24:49; Acts 1:4), also enables us to accept and accomplish the task of being a witness. In fact, one of the evidences of the Holy Spirit's presence is that we do become witnesses. As we see in Acts 1:8 and in Luke 24:48-49, Jesus promised that with the Holy Spirit would come "power." Furthermore, he said that when this occurs, the disciples "shall be" his witnesses. The implication is that a cause-and-effect relationship will take place. The

Holy Spirit with his accompanying power is the cause, and the effect is that the recipients of this power would be "witnesses."

The Greek word expressed as power in Acts 1:8—"you shall receive power"—is *dunamis*. This word, which is the root of the English words "dynamic" and "dynamite," means "inherent ability," "might," "power in action," and "miraculous power." These are significant words of empowerment designed to equip us to perform a very specific task: to be witnesses to Jesus Christ. If the world is to know and believe that Jesus is the Son of God with power to overcome the world and the things of the world, if they are to know that he has the power to overcome the effects of sin and death and the power to grant eternal life, then the message needs to be packaged in lives that demonstrate this overcoming power.

Unfortunately, many of us view the Holy Spirit simply as a concept and doctrinal tenet to which we profess belief rather than an active power and presence in our life and upon whom we can rely. Yet almost without exception, the more than ninety-five references to the Holy Spirit in the New Testament speak of his doing some action to us or for us. For instance, the Spirit is given to seal, sanctify, comfort, teach, guide, gift, empower, and send us. He is always an active presence.

Equally interesting is the fact that our relationship with the Holy Spirit is dependent upon our actions, as well. As we see again throughout the New Testament, we are to receive, believe, be filled with, and yield to the Holy Spirit, and we are cautioned not to quench, grieve, resist, or lie to him.

The Holy Spirit is real and active, and there is a dynamic interaction between each of us and the Holy Spirit that either enables him to have a growing influence in our life or diminishes his influence in our life. Consequently, a question we should ask ourselves in response to this truth is, "Am I more in tune with and yielding to the Holy Spirit's influence in my life today than I was a week, a month, or a year ago?"

The ascension of Jesus underscores not only the task of evangelization but the means of evangelization: the Holy Spirit, the promise of the Father, power from on high.

▶Learning from Scripture

1. Jesus instructed his disciples to wait for the promised Spirit (Luke 24:49; Acts 1:4). Review John 14:12-18, 26; 15:26-27; 16:7-17.
   a. What does the promise entail?

   _____

   _____

   _____

   _____

   _____

   _____

   _____

   b. What is the provision for fulfilling the promise?

   _____

   _____

   _____

   _____

   _____

   _____

   _____

c. What is the purpose behind the promise?

_____

_____

_____

_____

_____

_____

d. How is the purpose expressed in Acts 1:3-9?

_____

_____

_____

_____

_____

_____

e. What are the ramifications of this promise, not only for these disciples but also for individual Christians today and for the church?

_____

_____

_____

_____

_____

_____

2. Jesus told his disciples to preach his name "to all nations" (Luke 24:47) and to be his witnesses "in Jerusalem and in all Judea and Samaria and to the end of the earth" (Acts 1:8).

a. What are the ramifications of the commission's geographic parameters?

_____

_____

_____

_____

_____

_____

b. How do these geographic parameters apply to you personally?

_____

_____

_____

_____

_____

c. Was this commission given to these specific disciples as representative of the church or as representative of the individual Christian? What difference would it make?

_____

_____

_____

_____

_____

_____

3. Luke states that Jesus "opened [the disciples'] minds to understand the Scriptures" (Luke 24:45; see also 24:27, 32).
a. After reviewing John 14:20-26 and 16:12-15, explain how our minds and understanding are opened to the Scriptures now.

_____

_____

_____

_____

_____

_____

b. To what extent do you feel that your mind has been opened to understanding the Scriptures? What can we do to enhance and encourage this experience?

_____

_____

_____

_____

_____

_____

4. Acts of the Apostles provides some wonderful examples of how the power of the Holy Spirit is at work in followers of Jesus. Read the following passages and identify the ways in which the Holy Spirit's power is manifested. Also indicate the purpose for which it was made known.
a. Acts 4:13-22, 31

_____

_____

_____

b. Acts 4:32-37

_____

_____

_____

_____

_____

_____

_____

c. Acts 6:8-10; 7:54-60

_____

_____

_____

_____

_____

_____

d. Acts 9:32-43

_____

_____

_____

_____

_____

_____

5. What effects of the Holy Spirit's indwelling have you experienced in your life? What effects of his power?

_____

_____

_____

_____

_____

_____

▶ Reflecting on the Church's Wisdom

He [Jesus] ascends into heaven, accompanied by the eyes of the disciples gazing after him. He lets them observe it, and he makes them witnesses. . . . They certainly saw, touched, and felt him. They confirmed their faith by looking at him and touching him. They accompanied him with their gaze as he ascends into heaven. With attentive ears, they heard the angel's voice assuring them and foretelling that Christ would come again. . . .

Neither sight alone nor handling of the Lord's limbs was still enough to ensure that they would become witnesses of Christ and bravely endure everything for the preaching of the truth, fighting against falsehood even to the shedding of their blood. Who gave them such capability? Listen to the Lord himself. "Stay in the city until you are clothed with power from on high." "You have seen and touched, but you are still not able to preach and die for what you have seen and touched, until you are clothed with power from on high."

—**St. Augustine,** Sermon 265D.6

Reflect on an occasion when you felt empowered by the Holy Spirit for service or ministry. What happened as you responded to the Spirit?

_____

_____

_____

_____

_____

_____

▶Living the Words of the Resurrection

The Holy Spirit only requires our responsiveness and cooperation to begin the process of filling our life and fashioning it to conform to the image and character of Christ. All we need to do is to exercise the actions mentioned above—to believe, to receive, to yield—and the Spirit will fulfill his part to sanctify, comfort, teach, guide, gift, empower, and send us. Each day through prayer and yielding to God, we can open our life to an ongoing Pentecost experience in which the Holy Spirit's power and presence will continually become more real and active in our life.

Set aside a few hours this week to visit a Catholic bookstore or to search online for one or two resources that could help you experience the fullness of the promised Holy Spirit that you received in baptism and confirmation.

▶Praying in Response to Jesus' Words

Write your own prayer to Jesus in response to his promise to send the
Holy Spirit to us.

_____

_____

_____

_____

_____

_____

_____

▶Prayer Together

Pray the following prayer daily during the week prior to discussing
this chapter, then close your discussion by praying it in unison:

Breathe in me, O Holy Spirit,
That my thoughts may all be holy.

Act in me, O Holy Spirit,
That my work, too, may be holy.

Draw my heart, O Holy Spirit,
That I love but what is holy.

Strengthen me, O Holy Spirit,
To defend all that is holy.

Guard me, then, O Holy Spirit,
That I always may be holy.
—**St. Augustine,** *The Catholic Source Book*

Chapter 8

*"Go and make disciples
of all nations."*

Matthew 28:16-20

16 Now the eleven disciples went to Galilee, to the mountain to which Jesus had directed them. 17And when they saw him they worshiped him; but some doubted. 18And Jesus came and said to them, "All authority in heaven and on earth has been given to me. 19Go therefore and make disciples of all nations, baptizing them in the name of the Father and of the Son and of the Holy Spirit, 20teaching them to observe all that I have commanded you; and lo, I am with you always, to the close of the age."

Mark 16:14-20

14 [Jesus] appeared to the eleven themselves as they sat at table; and he upbraided them for their unbelief and hardness of heart, because they had not believed those who saw him after he had risen. 15And he said to them, "Go into all the world and preach the gospel to the whole creation. 16He who believes and is baptized will be saved; but he who does not believe will be condemned. 17And these signs will accompany those who believe: in my name they will cast out demons; they will speak in new tongues; 18they will pick up serpents, and if they drink any deadly thing, it will not hurt them; they will lay their hands on the sick, and they will recover."

19 So then the Lord Jesus, after he had spoken to them, was taken up into heaven, and sat down at the right hand of God. 20And they went forth and preached everywhere, while the Lord worked with them and confirmed the message by the signs that attended it. Amen.

G o therefore and make disciples of all nations" (Matthew 28:19)—the commission that Jesus gave to the apostles before he ascended into heaven is his master plan for reaching all of humankind with the good news. With this mandate to his first disciples, he set in motion his strategy by which generation after generation of followers would continue to spread the gospel to "the whole creation" (Mark 16:15), to generation after generation of men and women anywhere and everywhere who are hungry for truth and eternal life.

Jesus' plan for reaching the world gives Christians their formal "marching orders" and authorization to act, their commission to represent him and his kingdom in the world—a lifetime commission, by the way. Pope Paul VI described this mandate as "a duty incumbent . . . by the command of the Lord Jesus, so that people can believe and be saved" (*Evangelii nuntiandi,* 5). Pope John Paul II warned that "no believer in Christ, no institution of the Church can avoid this supreme duty: to proclaim Christ to all peoples" (*Redemptoris Missio,* 3). Jesus gave the first command, and the church has continued to reiterate it. Clearly, it is a command we cannot ignore.

Each of us has an individual responsibility to use our gifts and talents to fulfill the commission we have been given. But many of us may respond in dismay and fear, bemoaning the fact that we are shy, or inarticulate, or unlearned, or for a host of other reasons cannot witness for Christ. But the beauty of this Great Commission is that it excludes no one and includes all. The commission was given to the church, and so its fulfillment rests not on any one individual but on the community at large. Combined with those of the rest of the church, our talents—however meager they may seem to us—are more than adequate for the task.

Within the command itself, we see the reason why it takes *all* the members of the church to fulfill it. The command is to make disciples, baptizing them and teaching them. The first step of this "three-step process" involves us, described by Pope John Paul II as a "countless number of lay people, both women and men, busy at work in their daily life and activity, oftentimes far from view and quite unacclaimed by the world, . . . looked upon in love by the Father, untiring laborers who work in the Lord's vineyard" (*Christifideles Laici,* 17). Our command to "go" does not normally mean to other lands but to the people we encounter in our daily life and activities. There, our good deeds and righteous living adorn the gospel and cause people to ask in many different ways, "Why are you like you are?" Then, having established relationships and whetted their appetites for Christ, we can proclaim "the name, the teaching, the life, the promises, the Kingdom and the mystery of Jesus of Nazareth, the Son of God" (*Evangelii nuntiandi,* 22). It should not be a scary thing, nor should we need a seminary education, to tell a hungry soul about a friend we call Jesus.

Carrying out the second step—"baptizing them in the name of the Father and of the Son and of the Holy Spirit" (Matthew 28:19)—is normally the responsibility of priests and deacons, the ordained clergy. Finally, both clergy and laity become involved helping these new believers understand what Christ's teachings mean and how to follow them (see 28:20), including the responsibility to "go" to their world. In this way Jesus' master plan is continually being carried out.

In theological terms, this three-step process involves enabling people to experience conversion to Christ, transformation in Christ, and mobilization for Christ. It takes a team effort and provides wonderful rewards. For not only do we see lives rescued and changed in Christ, but we experience Jesus in new and deeper ways, for he promised, "I am with you to the close of the age" (Matthew 28:20). Do you want to draw close to Christ? Then try sharing his love with others.

Let's look more deeply now at various aspects of the task Jesus has given us.

►Learning from Scripture

1. How do you respond to the mandate from Jesus in Matthew 28:19-20?

    _____

    _____

    _____

    _____

    _____

    _____

    _____

2. What additional information and insights does Mark 16:15-18 add to Jesus' mandate as recorded by Matthew?

    _____

    _____

    _____

    _____

    _____

    _____

3. Define in your own words what the following two commands should mean to an ordinary Christian:
    a. "Go into all the world."

    _____

    _____

    _____

    _____

    _____

b. "Preach the gospel."

_____

_____

_____

_____

_____

_____

_____

4. Why is proclaiming the gospel so necessary?

_____

_____

_____

_____

_____

_____

5. Read and reflect on 2 Corinthians 5:17-21.
    a. In this passage, how does St. Paul express the gospel mandate?

_____

_____

_____

_____

_____

_____

b. Who or what is being reconciled? Why is reconciliation necessary?

_____

_____

_____

_____

_____

_____

c. Using your own words, how would you describe the responsibilities given to us in this passage?

_____

_____

_____

_____

_____

_____

d. What are the elements of the good news according to this passage?

_____

_____

_____

_____

_____

_____

6. Mark 16:16 indicates a very serious consequence of not believing the gospel. What do the Scriptures and the church teach about "condemnation"? Read John 3:16-21 and 1033–1034 in the *Catechism of the Catholic Church* to help you respond to this question.

_____

_____

_____

_____

_____

_____

_____

7. Describe three things that would enable you to become a more effective participant in taking the gospel to your world.

_____

_____

_____

_____

_____

_____

_____

▶Reflecting on the Church's Wisdom

The lay faithful, precisely because they are members of the Church, have the vocation and mission of proclaiming the Gospel: they are prepared for this work by the sacraments of Christian initiation and by the gifts of the Holy Spirit. . . .

The entire mission of the Church, then, is concentrated and manifested in evangelization. Through the winding passages of history the Church has made her way under the grace and the command of Jesus Christ: "Go into all the world and preach the gospel to the whole creation" (Mark 16:15) . . . "and lo, I am with you always, until the close of the age" (Matthew 28:20). "To evangelize," writes Paul VI, "is the grace and vocation proper to the Church, her most profound identity."

Certainly the command of Jesus: "Go and preach the Gospel" always maintains its vital value and its ever-pressing obligation. Nevertheless, *the present situation,* not only of the world but also of many parts of the Church, *absolutely demands that the word of Christ receive a more ready and generous obedience.* Every disciple is personally called by name; no disciple can withhold making a response: "Woe to me, if I do not preach the gospel" (1 Corinthians 9:16).

—**Pope John Paul II,** *Christifideles Laici,* 33

As a member of the church, how are you carrying out your vocation and mission to proclaim the gospel?

_____

_____

_____

_____

_____

_____

_____

▶Living the Words of the Resurrection

As a young university student studying speech communication, I quickly learned that the old sayings "actions speak more loudly than words" and "a picture is worth a thousand words" are more than mere clichés. Actions and visual aids go a long way in reinforcing verbal communication.

Jesus may have had this in mind when he said, "Let your light so shine before men, that they may see your good works and give glory to your Father who is in heaven" (Matthew 5:16). Witnessing for Christ encompasses both word and deed; in fact, St. Paul says that our deeds "adorn the doctrine of God our Savior" (Titus 2:10). Without deeds, our words may often seem sterile and academic, sometimes even harsh, whereas without the proclamation of Jesus and the good news our deeds may often be ineffective in pointing others to Christ and salvation.

May God open our eyes and heart to see opportunities each day to do good, and give us the courage to speak words of hope to those around us.

▶Praying in Response to Jesus' Words

Write a prayer to Jesus expressing your feelings and desires about participating in the Great Commission (see Matthew 28:16-20).

_____

_____

_____

_____

_____

_____

_____

▶Prayer Together

Pray the following prayer daily during the week prior to discussing this chapter, then close your group discussion by praying it in unison:

God our Father,
You called us each by name
And gave Your only Son to redeem us.
In Your faithfulness, You sent the Holy Spirit
To complete the mission of Jesus among us.

Open our hearts to Jesus
Give us the courage to speak His name
To those who are close to us
And the generosity to share His love
With those who are far away.

We pray that every person
throughout the world
Would be invited to know and love Jesus
as Savior and Redeemer.
May they come to know His unsurpassing love.
May that love transform every element of our society.
We make this prayer
through our Lord Jesus Christ, Your Son,
Who lives and reigns with you and the Holy Spirit,
One God, forever and ever. Amen
    —Official prayer of the Office of Evangelization 2000 throughout the decade dedicated to Catholic evangelization, December 25, 1990—December 25, 2000

Sources and Acknowledgments

Augustine of Hippo. *The Catholic Source Book*. Orlando, FL: Harcourt Religion Publishers, 2000.

Augustine of Hippo. Sermon 265D.6, *Ancient Christian Commentary on Scripture,* vol. III, Edited by Arthur A. Just, Jr. Downers Grove, IL: Intervarsity Press, 2003.

Bonhoeffer, Dietrich. *Life Together.* New York: Harper and Row, 1954.

Cyril of Jerusalem. *Liturgy of the Hours.* New York: Catholic Book Publishing Company, 1975.

Guardini, Romano. *The Lord.* Washington, DC: Regnery Publishing, Inc., 1982.

John Paul II. *A Gift of Enduring Love.* Chicago: Loyola Press, 2003.

John Paul II. Apostolic Exhortation on Reconciliation and Penance in the Mission of the Church Today (*Reconciliatio et Paenitentia*), 2 December 1984. http://www.vatican.va/holy_father/john_paul_ii/apost_exhortations/documents/hf_jp-ii_exh_02121984_reconciliatio-et-paenitentia_en.html.

John Paul II. Message for the 42nd World Day of Prayer for Vocations, 17 April 2005. http://www.vatican.va/holy_father/john_paul_ii/messages/vocations/documents/hf_jp-ii_mes_20040811_xlii-voc-2005_en.html.

John Paul II. Apostolic Exhortation on the Vocation and the Mission of the Lay Faithful in the Church and in the World (*Christifideles Laici*), 30 December 1988. http://www.vatican.va/holy_father/john_paul_ii/apost_exhortations/documents/hf_jp-ii_exh_30121988_christifideles-laici_en.html.

John Paul II. Encyclical Letter on the Permanent Validity of the Church's Missionary Mandate (*Redemptoris Missio*), 7 December 1990. http://www.vatican.va/holy_father/john_paul_ii/encyclicals/documents/hf_jp-ii_enc_07121990_redemptoris-missio_en.html.

Kempis, Thomas à. *The Imitation of Christ.* Translated by Leo Sherley-Price. New York: Dorset Press, 1986.

LaVerdiere, Eugene. *Dining in the Kingdom of God.* Chicago: Liturgy Training Publications, 1994.

Official prayer of the Office of Evangelization 2000 throughout the decade dedicated to Catholic evangelization, December 25, 1990—December 25, 2000. http://www.evangelization2000.org/let_us_pray.htm.

Origen. "On First Principles I.3." *Ancient Christian Commentary on Scripture, Volume II.* Edited by T. C. Oden and C. A. Hall. Downers Grove, IL: Intervarsity Press, 1998.

Paul VI. Apostolic Exhortation to the Episcopate, to the Clergy and to All the Faithful of the Entire World *(Evangelii nuntiandi),* 8 December 1975. http://www.vatican.va/holy_father/paul_vi/apost_exhortations/documents/hf_p-vi_exh_19751208_evangelii-nuntiandi_en.html.

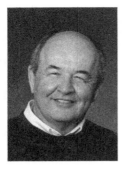

About the Author

Rich Cleveland and his wife, Gail, have been involved in ministry since 1974. Rich has served in several leadership positions at Holy Apostles Parish in Colorado Springs, Colorado, including as director of the Small Christian Communities Ministry. He and his wife have three grown children.

Rich also is director of Emmaus Journey: Catholic Small Group Ministry. Through this ministry, Rich and Gail have published several Scripture-based Catholic small-group studies. Additionally, Rich publishes *Reflecting on Sunday's Readings*, a small-group study based on each Sunday's Mass readings, which can be downloaded for free from the Emmaus Journey Web site at www.emmausjourney.org.

Rich has served as speaker and seminar leader at numerous national Christian conferences and conventions, including the Franciscan University of Steubenville's Men's Conference, the National Council of Catholic Evangelization, and St. Paul's Institute of Evangelical Catholic Ministry.